Breaking Barriers: Navigating Autism With Therapeutic Insight

Travis Breeding

Published by Travis Breeding, 2024.

BREAKING BARRIERS: NAVIGATING AUTISM WITH THERAPEUTIC INSIGHT

First edition. February 19, 2024.

ISBN: 979-8223155249

Written by Travis Breeding.

Also by Travis Breeding

Harmony in Flux: Navigating Bi-Polar Brilliance
The Friendship Rainbow
The Great Kindergarten Adventure: A Story about Going to School
with Autism
The Magic Forest Adventure
Unlocking Brilliance: Navigating Autism and Applied Behavior
Analysis Towards a Radiant Future
Decoding Love: Navigating Dating and Relationships on the Autism
Spectrum
Echoes of a Late Diagnosis: Unveiling the Spectrum Within
From Theory to Practice: Implementing Effective Autism Interventions
St
The Amazing Adventures of Aiden and His Asperger's Superpowers
The Magical Adventures of Lily and the Enchanted Forest
Unlocking Potential: A Journey Of Discovery Through ABA Therapy
Unlocking Potential: Navigating Employment for Neurodiverse Talent
Unlocking the Spectrum: A Journey through Applied Behavior Analysis
from an Autistic Perspective
Unlocking The Spectrum: Navigating The Complexity Of Autism With
Advanced Strategies And Insights
Beyond The Spectrum: Insights From Autistic Adults
Beyond The Stereotypes
Breaking Barriers: Navigating Autism With Therapeutic Insight
Celebrating Neurodiversity
Embracing Differences

From Diagnosis To Treatment
From Dreams To Reality: The Young President
Living With Autism: A Journey Of Triumph And Challenges
Neurodiversity Unveiled: Navigating The Spectrum Of Inclusion
The Art Of Reinforcement
ThroughThe Spectrum Of Love

Watch for more at breedingautismconsulting.com.

Table of Contents

Chapter 1: Breaking Down Barriers: The Benefits of Speech Therapy for Children on the Autism Spectrum

Autism Spectrum Disorder (ASD) is a neurodevelopmental disorder that affects communication, social interaction, and behavior. It is characterized by a range of symptoms and can vary in severity from person to person. ASD is typically diagnosed in early childhood, although some individuals may not receive a diagnosis until later in life.

Common characteristics of ASD include difficulties with social interaction and communication, repetitive behaviors and interests, and sensory sensitivities. Children with ASD may have difficulty understanding and using language, making eye contact, and engaging in reciprocal conversation. They may also exhibit repetitive behaviors such as hand-flapping or rocking, and may have sensory sensitivities to certain sounds, textures, or lights.

The Importance of Early Intervention for Children with ASD

Early intervention is crucial for children with ASD as it can greatly improve their developmental outcomes. Research has shown that children who receive early intervention services have better long-term outcomes in terms of communication skills, social interaction, and behavior.

Early intervention can help children with ASD develop important skills that will benefit them throughout their lives. It can help improve their communication skills, social interaction abilities, and overall quality of life. Early intervention can also help reduce the severity of symptoms and improve the child's ability to function in everyday life.

Parents and caregivers play a critical role in early intervention for children with ASD. They are often the first to notice signs of ASD and can play a key role in seeking a diagnosis and accessing appropriate services. Parents and caregivers can also provide support and encouragement to their child during therapy sessions and help reinforce the skills learned in therapy at home.

The Role of Speech Therapy in Treating ASD

Speech therapy plays a crucial role in the treatment of ASD. It focuses on improving communication skills, including both verbal and nonverbal communication. Speech therapists work with children with ASD to help them develop language skills, improve their ability to understand and use language, and enhance their overall communication abilities.

Speech therapy for children with ASD is individualized and tailored to meet the specific needs of each child. It may include a variety of techniques and strategies to address the unique challenges that children with ASD face in communication. Speech therapists may use visual supports, such as pictures or visual schedules, to help children understand and follow instructions. They may also use play-based activities to engage children and make therapy sessions fun and motivating.

The goals of speech therapy for children with ASD are to improve their ability to communicate effectively, increase their understanding of language, and enhance their social interaction skills. Speech therapists work with children to help them develop functional communication skills that will enable them to express their wants and needs, engage in social interactions, and participate in everyday activities.

Speech Therapy Techniques for Children with ASD

There are several speech therapy techniques that have been found to be effective in treating ASD. These techniques are designed to address the specific communication challenges that children with ASD face and help them develop the skills they need to communicate effectively.

One technique commonly used in speech therapy for children with ASD is Applied Behavior Analysis (ABA). ABA focuses on teaching new skills and reducing problem behaviors by breaking them down into smaller, manageable steps. It uses positive reinforcement to encourage desired behaviors and helps children with ASD learn new skills through repetition and practice.

Another technique used in speech therapy for children with ASD is the Picture Exchange Communication System (PECS). PECS uses pictures or symbols to help children communicate their wants and needs. Children are taught to exchange a picture or symbol for an item or activity they desire, which helps them develop functional communication skills.

Social Stories are another technique used in speech therapy for children with ASD. Social Stories are short narratives that describe social situations or behaviors in a way that is easy for children with ASD to understand. They can help children learn appropriate social behaviors and understand the expectations of different social situations.

Visual Schedules are also commonly used in speech therapy for children with ASD. Visual schedules provide a visual representation of the sequence of activities or tasks that will occur throughout the day. They help children with ASD understand and anticipate what will happen next, which can reduce anxiety and improve their ability to transition between activities.

Improving Communication Skills through Speech Therapy

Speech therapy can greatly improve the communication skills of children with ASD. By working with a speech therapist, children can learn to understand and use language more effectively, express their wants and needs, and engage in meaningful conversations.

There are several strategies that speech therapists use to improve communication skills in children with ASD. One strategy is to focus on functional communication, which means teaching children to use language to express their wants and needs in everyday situations. This can include teaching them to request items or activities, ask for help, or initiate social interactions.

Another strategy is to use visual supports to enhance communication. Visual supports, such as pictures or visual schedules, can help children with ASD understand and follow instructions, as well as communicate their wants and needs. Visual supports can also help children with ASD develop a better understanding of language and improve their ability to express themselves.

Speech therapists also work on improving the social communication skills of children with ASD. This includes teaching them how to engage in reciprocal conversations, take turns during conversations, and understand nonverbal cues such as body language and facial expressions. By improving their social communication skills, children with ASD can better navigate social interactions and build meaningful relationships.

Enhancing Social Interaction and Play Skills

Speech therapy can also play a crucial role in enhancing the social interaction and play skills of children with ASD. Many children with

ASD struggle with social interaction and may have difficulty engaging in age-appropriate play activities.

Speech therapists work with children to help them develop the social skills they need to interact with others and engage in play activities. This can include teaching them how to initiate and maintain conversations, take turns during play, and understand social cues. Speech therapists may also use play-based activities to help children practice these skills in a fun and motivating way.

Strategies for enhancing social interaction and play skills in children with ASD can include using visual supports, such as social stories or visual schedules, to help them understand the expectations of different social situations or play activities. Speech therapists may also use role-playing or video modeling to help children learn and practice appropriate social behaviors.

By enhancing their social interaction and play skills, children with ASD can improve their ability to form friendships, engage in cooperative play, and participate in social activities. This can greatly enhance their overall quality of life and help them develop important social skills that will benefit them throughout their lives.

Addressing Behavioral Challenges with Speech Therapy

Children with ASD often face behavioral challenges that can impact their ability to communicate effectively and engage in social interactions. Speech therapy can play a crucial role in addressing these behavioral challenges and helping children develop more appropriate behaviors.

Speech therapists work with children to identify the underlying causes of problem behaviors and develop strategies to address them. This may include teaching children alternative ways to communicate their wants and needs, such as using pictures or symbols, or teaching them self-regulation techniques to manage their emotions.

One technique commonly used in speech therapy for addressing behavioral challenges is the use of visual supports. Visual supports can help children understand and follow instructions, as well as provide a visual reminder of appropriate behaviors. They can also help children with ASD anticipate and prepare for transitions or changes in routine, which can reduce anxiety and prevent problem behaviors.

Another technique used in speech therapy for addressing behavioral challenges is the use of social stories. Social stories can help children with ASD understand appropriate behaviors in different social situations and provide them with strategies for managing challenging behaviors. By teaching children alternative ways to respond to challenging situations, speech therapists can help them develop more appropriate behaviors and improve their overall functioning.

The Benefits of Speech Therapy for School-Aged Children with ASD

Speech therapy continues to be beneficial for school-aged children with ASD. It can help improve their academic success, social interaction skills, and overall quality of life.

In the school setting, speech therapy can help children with ASD develop the communication skills they need to participate in classroom activities, understand and follow instructions, and engage in meaningful conversations with peers and teachers. Speech therapists can also work with teachers and other school staff to develop strategies and accommodations to support the child's communication needs in the classroom.

Speech therapy can also help improve the social interaction skills of school-aged children with ASD. By working with a speech therapist, children can learn how to initiate and maintain conversations, understand social cues, and navigate social situations. This can greatly enhance their ability to form friendships, participate in group activities, and engage in cooperative play.

In addition to improving communication and social interaction skills, speech therapy can also help address behavioral challenges that may arise in the school setting. By teaching children alternative ways to communicate their wants and needs, as well as strategies for managing challenging behaviors, speech therapists can help children with ASD succeed academically and socially.

Speech Therapy for Nonverbal Children with ASD

Speech therapy can be particularly beneficial for nonverbal children with ASD. Nonverbal children have difficulty using spoken language to communicate and may rely on alternative forms of communication, such as gestures or pictures.

Speech therapists work with nonverbal children to help them develop functional communication skills. This may include teaching them alternative ways to communicate their wants and needs, such as using pictures or symbols. Speech therapists may also use augmentative and alternative communication (AAC) devices, such as tablets or communication boards, to help nonverbal children communicate more effectively.

Strategies for improving communication skills in nonverbal children with ASD can include using visual supports, such as visual schedules or social stories, to help them understand and follow instructions. Speech therapists may also use play-based activities to engage nonverbal children and help them practice using alternative forms of communication.

By improving their communication skills, nonverbal children with ASD can better express their wants and needs, engage in social interactions, and participate in everyday activities. This can greatly enhance their overall quality of life and improve their ability to function in different environments.

Working with Families to Support Speech Therapy Goals

Family involvement is crucial in supporting the goals of speech therapy for children with ASD. Parents and caregivers play a key role in helping their child develop and practice the skills learned in therapy.

Speech therapists work closely with families to provide education and support. They may provide strategies and techniques for parents to use at home to reinforce the skills learned in therapy. They may also provide resources and information to help parents better understand their child's communication needs and how to support their development.

It is important for families to be actively involved in the therapy process. This can include attending therapy sessions, participating in parent training programs, and practicing the skills learned in therapy at home. By working together with the speech therapist, families can help their child make progress towards their communication goals and improve their overall functioning.

The Positive Impact of Speech Therapy on Children with ASD

Speech therapy plays a crucial role in the treatment of Autism Spectrum Disorder (ASD). It can help children with ASD develop important communication skills, improve their social interaction abilities, and address behavioral challenges.

Early intervention is key in maximizing the benefits of speech therapy for children with ASD. By starting therapy early, children can develop important skills that will benefit them throughout their lives. Parents and caregivers also play a critical role in early intervention by seeking a diagnosis and accessing appropriate services.

Speech therapy techniques such as Applied Behavior Analysis (ABA), Picture Exchange Communication System (PECS), Social Stories, and Visual Schedules have been found to be effective in treating ASD. These techniques are designed to address the unique communication challenges that children with ASD face and help them develop the skills they need to communicate effectively.

Speech therapy can greatly improve the communication skills, social interaction abilities, and overall quality of life of children with ASD. By working with a speech therapist, children can develop the skills they need to navigate social interactions, engage in meaningful conversations, and participate in everyday activities. Family involvement is crucial in supporting the goals of speech therapy and helping children with ASD make progress towards their communication goals.

Chapter 2: Unlocking the Potential: How Occupational Therapy Can Help Children with Autism

Autism is a neurodevelopmental disorder that affects a child's social interaction, communication skills, and behavior. It is characterized by repetitive behaviors, difficulty with social interactions, and challenges with verbal and nonverbal communication. Autism can have a significant impact on a child's development, making it difficult for them to participate in everyday activities and reach their full potential.

Occupational therapy is a profession that focuses on helping individuals develop the skills they need to participate in meaningful activities. For children with autism, occupational therapy plays a crucial role in supporting their development and helping them overcome the challenges they face. Occupational therapists work with children to address their unique needs and help them achieve their goals.

The Role of Occupational Therapy in Autism Treatment

Occupational therapy can address various areas of development that are affected by autism. These areas include sensory processing, fine motor skills, gross motor skills, social skills, communication, and emotional regulation. By targeting these areas, occupational therapists can help children with autism improve their overall functioning and enhance their quality of life.

In terms of sensory processing, many children with autism experience difficulties in processing sensory information from their environment. They may be hypersensitive or hyposensitive to certain sensory stimuli, such as touch, sound, or movement. Occupational therapists can help children with autism develop strategies to regulate their sensory responses and improve their ability to engage in daily activities.

Identifying Sensory Processing Issues in Children with Autism

Sensory processing issues are common among children with autism. These issues occur when the brain has difficulty receiving and responding to sensory information from the environment. This can lead to overstimulation or understimulation, resulting in challenges with attention, behavior, and overall functioning.

Signs and symptoms of sensory processing issues in children with autism may include hypersensitivity or hyposensitivity to certain sensory stimuli, such as loud noises or textures. They may also exhibit repetitive behaviors, such as rocking or hand-flapping, as a way to self-regulate their sensory experiences. Occupational therapists are trained to identify these sensory processing issues and develop appropriate interventions to address them.

Sensory Integration Therapy: A Key Component of Occupational Therapy for Autism

Sensory integration therapy is a key component of occupational therapy for children with autism. It is a specialized approach that focuses on helping children process and respond to sensory information in a more organized and adaptive manner. The goal of sensory integration therapy is to improve a child's ability to participate in daily activities and engage with their environment.

There are various techniques and strategies used in sensory integration therapy, including sensory diets, therapeutic brushing, and deep pressure activities. These interventions are designed to provide the child with the sensory input they need to regulate their responses and improve their overall functioning. Occupational therapists work closely with children and their families to develop individualized sensory integration plans that address their specific needs.

Developing Fine Motor Skills and Handwriting Abilities in Children with Autism

Fine motor skills refer to the ability to use the small muscles of the hands and fingers for tasks such as writing, cutting, and buttoning. Children with autism often struggle with fine motor skills, which can impact their ability to perform everyday activities independently.

Occupational therapists use various techniques to help children with autism develop their fine motor skills. These may include activities that focus on hand-eye coordination, finger strength, and dexterity. Therapists may also incorporate play-based activities that target specific fine motor skills, such as using tweezers or manipulating small objects.

Handwriting abilities are also an important aspect of fine motor skills development. Occupational therapists can work with children with autism to improve their handwriting through activities that focus on letter formation, pencil grip, and overall writing fluency. By addressing these areas, occupational therapy can help children with autism become more independent in their daily activities.

Improving Gross Motor Skills and Coordination in Children with Autism

Gross motor skills refer to the ability to use the large muscles of the body for tasks such as walking, running, and jumping. Children with autism often have difficulties with gross motor skills and coordination, which can impact their ability to participate in physical activities and sports.

Occupational therapists can help children with autism improve their gross motor skills through various interventions. These may include activities that focus on balance, coordination, and strength. Therapists may also incorporate play-based activities that target specific gross motor skills, such as kicking a ball or climbing on playground equipment.

By addressing these areas, occupational therapy can help children with autism become more confident and independent in their physical abilities. This can have a positive impact on their overall development and well-being.

Enhancing Social Skills and Communication through Occupational Therapy

Social skills and communication are areas that are often impacted by autism. Children with autism may struggle with understanding social cues, initiating and maintaining conversations, and developing meaningful relationships.

Occupational therapists play a crucial role in helping children with autism enhance their social skills and communication abilities. They use various techniques and strategies to teach children how to read social cues, engage in appropriate conversations, and develop social relationships. These interventions may include role-playing activities, social stories, and group therapy sessions.

By addressing these areas, occupational therapy can help children with autism improve their social interactions and communication skills. This can have a significant impact on their ability to participate in school, make friends, and navigate social situations.

Addressing Behavioral Challenges and Emotional Regulation in Children with Autism

Behavioral challenges and emotional regulation difficulties are common among children with autism. They may exhibit behaviors such as tantrums, aggression, or self-stimulatory behaviors as a way to cope with their environment or express their needs.

Occupational therapists are trained to address these behavioral challenges and support children with autism in developing appropriate coping strategies. They work closely with children and their families to identify triggers for challenging behaviors and develop strategies to manage them. This may include teaching children relaxation techniques, providing sensory-based interventions, or implementing visual supports.

By addressing these areas, occupational therapy can help children with autism develop more effective coping strategies and improve their emotional regulation. This can lead to a reduction in challenging behaviors and an overall improvement in their quality of life.

Collaborating with Families and Caregivers to Support Children with Autism

Collaboration between occupational therapists, families, and caregivers is essential in supporting children with autism. Occupational therapists work closely with families to understand the unique needs of the child and develop individualized intervention plans.

Occupational therapists provide education and support to families, helping them understand the challenges their child faces and how they can support their development at home. They also collaborate with other professionals involved in the child's care, such as speech therapists or behavior analysts, to ensure a holistic approach to treatment.

By working together, occupational therapists, families, and caregivers can create a supportive environment that promotes the child's development and well-being.

The Importance of Early Intervention in Occupational Therapy for Autism

Early intervention is crucial in supporting children with autism. Research has shown that early intervention can lead to significant improvements in a child's development and long-term outcomes.

Occupational therapy plays a vital role in early intervention for children with autism. By identifying and addressing developmental challenges early on, occupational therapists can help children develop the skills they need to participate in everyday activities and reach their full potential.

Early intervention strategies may include sensory integration therapy, fine motor skills development, gross motor skills development, social skills training, and behavioral interventions. By implementing these strategies early on, occupational therapists can help children with autism overcome challenges and improve their overall functioning.

Unlocking the Potential of Children with Autism through Occupational Therapy

Occupational therapy plays a crucial role in supporting the development of children with autism. By addressing sensory processing issues, fine motor skills, gross motor skills, social skills, communication, and emotional regulation, occupational therapists can help children with autism overcome challenges and reach their full potential.

Through collaboration with families and caregivers, occupational therapists can create a supportive environment that promotes the child's development and well-being. Early intervention is key in supporting children with autism, and occupational therapy provides the necessary tools and strategies to help them thrive.

By unlocking the potential of children with autism through occupational therapy, we can ensure that they have the skills and abilities they need to lead fulfilling lives and participate fully in their communities.

Chapter 3 The Science Behind Behavioral Therapy for Autism: Explained

Autism is a neurodevelopmental disorder that affects social interaction, communication, and behavior. It is typically diagnosed in early childhood and can have a significant impact on an individual's daily functioning and quality of life. Behavioral therapy is a widely used approach for treating autism and helping individuals with autism develop new skills and reduce challenging behaviors.

Behavioral therapy is based on the principles of applied behavior analysis (ABA), which is a scientific approach to understanding and changing behavior. ABA focuses on identifying the underlying causes of behavior and using evidence-based strategies to promote positive behavior change. It is a highly individualized approach that takes into account the unique needs and strengths of each individual with autism.

The Principles of Applied Behavior Analysis

Applied behavior analysis (ABA) is the foundation of behavioral therapy for autism. It is a systematic approach to understanding and changing behavior that is based on the principles of behaviorism. The four main principles of ABA are:

1. Positive reinforcement: Positive reinforcement involves providing a reward or consequence that increases the likelihood of a desired behavior occurring again in the future. This can be done through the use of praise, tokens, or other rewards that are meaningful to the individual with autism.

2. Prompting: Prompting involves providing cues or assistance to help an individual with autism perform a desired behavior. Prompting can be physical, verbal, or visual, depending on the needs and abilities of the individual.

3. Generalization: Generalization involves teaching skills in multiple settings and with different people to ensure that the individual with autism can use those skills in a variety of situations. This helps to promote independence and flexibility in their behavior.

4. Data collection and analysis: Data collection and analysis are essential components of ABA. By collecting data on behaviors and interventions, therapists can track progress, make informed decisions about treatment, and evaluate the effectiveness of interventions.

The Role of Positive Reinforcement in Behavioral Therapy

Positive reinforcement is a key component of behavioral therapy for autism. It involves providing a reward or consequence that increases the likelihood of a desired behavior occurring again in the future. Positive reinforcement can be used to teach new skills, shape behavior, and reduce challenging behaviors.

In behavioral therapy, positive reinforcement is used to motivate individuals with autism to engage in desired behaviors. This can be done through the use of praise, tokens, or other rewards that are meaningful to the individual. For example, if a child with autism is learning to brush their teeth independently, they may receive a small reward, such as a sticker or a favorite toy, each time they successfully complete the task.

Positive reinforcement is effective because it helps individuals with autism associate desired behaviors with positive outcomes. Over time, this association strengthens and the desired behaviors become more likely to occur. By using positive reinforcement consistently and strategically, therapists can help individuals with autism develop new skills and reduce challenging behaviors.

The Importance of Data Collection and Analysis

Data collection and analysis are essential components of behavioral therapy for autism. By collecting data on behaviors and interventions, therapists can track progress, make informed decisions about treatment, and evaluate the effectiveness of interventions.

Data collection involves systematically recording information about the frequency, duration, and intensity of behaviors. This can be done using various methods, such as direct observation, interviews with parents and caregivers, and self-report measures. The data collected provides objective information about the individual's behavior and allows therapists to identify patterns and trends over time.

Data analysis involves analyzing the collected data to identify patterns, trends, and relationships between behaviors and interventions. This helps therapists make informed decisions about treatment strategies and evaluate the effectiveness of interventions. For example, if a child with autism is learning to communicate using sign language, data analysis may reveal that they are more likely to use signs when given verbal prompts or when provided with a specific reward.

By using data collection and analysis, therapists can tailor interventions to the specific needs and strengths of each individual with autism. This individualized approach is crucial for promoting positive behavior change and helping individuals with autism reach their full potential.

Techniques Used in Behavioral Therapy for Autism

There are several techniques used in behavioral therapy for autism, each with its own unique approach and focus. Some of the most commonly used techniques include:

1. Discrete trial training (DTT): DTT is a structured teaching method that breaks down skills into small, manageable steps. It involves presenting a stimulus or cue, prompting the desired response, and providing positive reinforcement for correct responses. DTT is often used to teach new skills, such as language and social skills.

2. Naturalistic teaching: Naturalistic teaching involves embedding teaching opportunities into everyday activities and routines. It focuses on promoting learning in naturalistic settings and using the individual's interests and motivations to drive learning. Naturalistic teaching is often

used to promote social interaction, play skills, and generalization of skills.

3. Pivotal response training (PRT): PRT is a child-centered approach that focuses on targeting pivotal areas of development, such as motivation, responsivity to multiple cues, self-management, and social initiations. It involves providing choices, using natural reinforcers, and promoting self-initiated behaviors. PRT is often used to promote language development, social skills, and independence.

These techniques are highly individualized and can be tailored to meet the specific needs and strengths of each individual with autism. They are evidence-based approaches that have been shown to be effective in promoting positive behavior change and skill development.

Strategies for Teaching New Skills

Teaching new skills is a key component of behavioral therapy for autism. There are several strategies that can be used to effectively teach new skills, including:

1. Task analysis: Task analysis involves breaking down complex skills into smaller, more manageable steps. This helps individuals with autism understand and learn the individual components of a skill before putting them together. For example, if a child with autism is learning to tie their shoes, task analysis may involve breaking the skill down into steps such as crossing the laces, making loops, and pulling the loops tight.

2. Prompting: Prompting involves providing cues or assistance to help an individual with autism perform a desired behavior. Prompting can be physical, verbal, or visual, depending on the needs and abilities of the individual. Prompting is gradually faded over time as the individual becomes more independent in performing the skill.

3. Generalization: Generalization involves teaching skills in multiple settings and with different people to ensure that the individual with autism can use those skills in a variety of situations. This helps to promote independence and flexibility in their behavior. For example, if a child with autism is learning to greet others, they may practice greeting different people in different settings, such as at home, at school, and in the community.

These strategies are effective in promoting skill development and helping individuals with autism generalize their skills to different settings and situations.

Addressing Challenging Behaviors with Behavioral Therapy

Challenging behaviors are common in individuals with autism and can have a significant impact on their daily functioning and quality of life. Behavioral therapy provides strategies for addressing challenging behaviors and promoting positive behavior change.

Challenging behaviors can include aggression, self-injury, tantrums, noncompliance, and repetitive behaviors. These behaviors often serve a specific function for the individual with autism, such as escaping a demand or gaining attention. Behavioral therapy focuses on understanding the underlying function of the behavior and addressing it through positive behavior change strategies.

Strategies for addressing challenging behaviors include:

1. Functional behavior assessment (FBA): FBA involves systematically gathering information about the antecedents (what happens before the behavior), the behavior itself, and the consequences (what happens after the behavior) of the challenging behavior. This helps to identify the function of the behavior and develop a targeted intervention plan.

2. Replacement behaviors: Replacement behaviors are alternative behaviors that serve the same function as the challenging behavior but are more socially appropriate. For example, if a child with autism engages in self-injurious behavior to escape a demand, a replacement behavior may be teaching them to request a break or use a visual schedule to indicate when they need a break.

3. Positive behavior support: Positive behavior support involves creating an environment that promotes positive behavior and reduces the likelihood of challenging behaviors occurring. This can include modifying the physical environment, providing clear expectations and routines, and teaching alternative coping strategies.

These strategies are individualized to meet the specific needs and strengths of each individual with autism. They focus on promoting positive behavior change and reducing the impact of challenging behaviors on daily functioning.

The Benefits of Early Intervention

Early intervention is crucial for individuals with autism as it can have a significant impact on their long-term outcomes. Research has consistently shown that early intervention leads to better outcomes in areas such as language development, social skills, and adaptive functioning.

Early intervention for autism typically involves behavioral therapy that is tailored to meet the unique needs and strengths of each individual. It focuses on promoting positive behavior change, teaching new skills, and reducing challenging behaviors.

The benefits of early intervention include:

1. Improved language development: Early intervention can help individuals with autism develop language skills and improve their ability

to communicate effectively. This can have a significant impact on their social interactions, academic performance, and overall quality of life.

2. Enhanced social skills: Early intervention can help individuals with autism develop social skills and improve their ability to interact with others. This can lead to increased opportunities for social engagement, friendships, and community participation.

3. Increased independence: Early intervention can help individuals with autism develop independence in daily living skills, such as self-care, household tasks, and community navigation. This can promote their overall functioning and reduce their reliance on others for support.

4. Reduced challenging behaviors: Early intervention can help individuals with autism reduce challenging behaviors and develop more adaptive coping strategies. This can improve their overall behavior and reduce the impact of challenging behaviors on their daily functioning.

Early intervention is most effective when it is started as soon as possible after a diagnosis of autism. It provides individuals with autism with the best chance for positive outcomes and a fulfilling life.

The Role of Parents and Caregivers in Behavioral Therapy

Parents and caregivers play a crucial role in the success of behavioral therapy for autism. Their involvement and support are essential for promoting positive behavior change and skill development.

The importance of parent and caregiver involvement in behavioral therapy includes:

1. Consistency: Parents and caregivers are often the primary caregivers for individuals with autism, so their consistency in implementing behavioral strategies is crucial. Consistency helps individuals with autism understand expectations, learn new skills, and generalize those skills to different settings and situations.

2. Generalization: Parents and caregivers can help promote generalization of skills by providing opportunities for practice in different settings and with different people. This helps individuals with autism transfer their skills from therapy sessions to real-life situations.

3. Reinforcement: Parents and caregivers can provide additional reinforcement for desired behaviors outside of therapy sessions. This helps to strengthen the association between the desired behavior and the positive outcome, making it more likely to occur in the future.

4. Advocacy: Parents and caregivers are often the strongest advocates for individuals with autism. They can work closely with therapists, educators, and other professionals to ensure that the individual's needs are met and that they have access to appropriate services and supports.

Strategies for involving parents and caregivers in behavioral therapy include providing training, resources, and ongoing support. This helps to empower parents and caregivers to effectively support their loved ones with autism and promote positive behavior change.

The Effectiveness of Behavioral Therapy for Autism

Research has consistently shown that behavioral therapy is an effective treatment for autism. Numerous studies have demonstrated its effectiveness in promoting positive behavior change, teaching new skills, and reducing challenging behaviors.

A meta-analysis of 27 studies on the effectiveness of behavioral therapy for autism found that it led to significant improvements in communication skills, social skills, and adaptive functioning. The analysis also found that the effects of behavioral therapy were maintained over time, suggesting that the benefits are long-lasting.

Success stories of individuals with autism who have benefited from behavioral therapy are also abundant. These stories highlight the positive impact that behavioral therapy can have on individuals with autism and their families. From learning to communicate effectively to gaining independence in daily living skills, individuals with autism have made significant progress through behavioral therapy.

Future Directions in Behavioral Therapy Research

Research in the field of behavioral therapy for autism is constantly evolving, with new studies and approaches being developed. Some current research trends include:

1.   Technology-based   interventions: Technology-based interventions, such as virtual reality and mobile applications, are being explored as potential tools for delivering behavioral therapy. These interventions have the potential to increase access to services and provide more personalized and engaging interventions.

2. Individualized approaches: There is a growing recognition of the importance of individualized approaches in behavioral therapy. Researchers are exploring ways to tailor interventions to meet the unique needs and strengths of each individual with autism, taking into account factors such as age, cognitive abilities, and interests.

3. Parent-mediated interventions: Parent-mediated interventions involve training parents to deliver behavioral therapy techniques at home. This approach recognizes the important role that parents play in the success of behavioral therapy and aims to empower them to effectively support their child's development.

Future directions in behavioral therapy research will continue to focus on improving outcomes for individuals with autism and identifying the most effective strategies for promoting positive behavior change and skill development.

Conclusion:

Behavioral therapy is a highly effective approach for treating autism and helping individuals with autism develop new skills and reduce challenging behaviors. It is based on the principles of applied behavior analysis (ABA) and focuses on understanding and changing behavior through positive reinforcement, data collection and analysis, and individualized interventions.

Parents and caregivers play a crucial role in the success of behavioral therapy, as their involvement and support are essential for promoting positive behavior change and skill development. Early intervention is also crucial for individuals with autism, as it leads to better outcomes in areas such as language development, social skills, and adaptive functioning.

Research on the effectiveness of behavioral therapy for autism is abundant, with numerous studies demonstrating its positive impact on individuals with autism and their families. Future directions in behavioral therapy research will continue to focus on improving outcomes and identifying the most effective strategies for promoting positive behavior change and skill development.

Parents and caregivers are encouraged to seek out behavioral therapy for their loved ones with autism, as it provides them with the best chance for positive outcomes and a fulfilling life. With the right support and interventions, individuals with autism can reach their full potential and thrive in all areas of life.

Chapter 4: Beyond the Basics: Advanced Interventions for Autism Spectrum Disorder

Autism Spectrum Disorder (ASD) is a neurodevelopmental disorder that affects individuals in various ways. It is characterized by difficulties in social interaction, communication, and repetitive behaviors. While there is no cure for ASD, there are advanced interventions available that can greatly improve the quality of life for individuals with this disorder. These interventions aim to address the specific challenges faced by individuals with ASD and help them develop skills and strategies to navigate the world more effectively.

Seeking advanced interventions for individuals with ASD is crucial because it can make a significant difference in their overall well-being and development. These interventions are designed to target the specific needs of individuals with ASD and provide them with the support and tools they need to thrive. By addressing the challenges associated with ASD early on, individuals can have a better chance of reaching their full potential and leading fulfilling lives.

Understanding Autism Spectrum Disorder and Its Challenges

Autism Spectrum Disorder is a complex neurodevelopmental disorder that affects individuals in different ways. It is characterized by difficulties in social interaction, communication, and repetitive behaviors. Individuals with ASD may have difficulty understanding social cues, expressing themselves verbally or non-verbally, and may engage in repetitive behaviors such as hand-flapping or rocking.

One of the main challenges faced by individuals with ASD is social interaction. They may struggle to understand social cues such as facial expressions, body language, and tone of voice. This can make it difficult for them to form meaningful relationships and navigate social situations effectively. Communication is another area of challenge for individuals with ASD. They may have difficulty expressing themselves verbally or understanding spoken language. This can lead to frustration and isolation.

Individualized interventions are crucial for individuals with ASD because each person's needs and challenges are unique. What works for one individual may not work for another. By tailoring interventions to the specific needs of each individual, professionals can provide targeted support that addresses their challenges and helps them develop the skills they need to succeed.

The Importance of Early Intervention and Diagnosis

Early intervention and diagnosis are crucial for individuals with ASD because they can greatly improve outcomes and quality of life. Research has shown that early intervention can lead to significant improvements in communication, social skills, and cognitive abilities for individuals with ASD. The earlier the intervention is provided, the better the chances of positive outcomes.

There are several signs and symptoms that may indicate the presence of ASD. These can include delayed speech or language skills, difficulty with social interactions, repetitive behaviors, and sensory sensitivities. It is important for parents and caregivers to be aware of these signs and seek professional help if they suspect their child may have ASD.

Seeking professional help for diagnosis and intervention is essential because it allows individuals with ASD to receive the support and resources they need to thrive. Professionals can conduct comprehensive assessments to determine if an individual has ASD and develop a personalized intervention plan based on their specific needs. Early intervention can provide individuals with the tools and strategies they need to navigate the challenges associated with ASD and reach their full potential.

Behavioral Interventions for Autism Spectrum Disorder

Behavioral interventions are a common approach used in the treatment of Autism Spectrum Disorder. These interventions focus on modifying behaviors and teaching new skills to individuals with ASD. They are based on the principles of applied behavior analysis (ABA) and aim to increase desired behaviors while decreasing challenging behaviors.

There are several examples of behavioral interventions that can be effective for individuals with ASD. One example is discrete trial training (DTT), which involves breaking down skills into smaller steps and using repetition and reinforcement to teach those skills. Another example is pivotal response training (PRT), which focuses on teaching pivotal skills such as motivation, self-management, and responding to multiple cues.

Behavioral interventions have been shown to have many benefits for individuals with ASD. They can help improve communication skills, social interactions, and adaptive behaviors. These interventions also provide individuals with the tools and strategies they need to navigate the challenges associated with ASD and lead more independent lives.

Cognitive Interventions for Autism Spectrum Disorder

Cognitive interventions focus on improving cognitive abilities such as attention, memory, problem-solving, and executive functioning in individuals with ASD. These interventions aim to enhance cognitive skills and help individuals with ASD develop strategies to overcome cognitive challenges.

There are several examples of cognitive interventions that can be effective for individuals with ASD. One example is cognitive behavioral therapy (CBT), which helps individuals identify and change negative thought patterns and behaviors. Another example is social thinking, which focuses on teaching individuals with ASD how to understand and interpret social cues.

Cognitive interventions have been shown to have many benefits for individuals with ASD. They can improve cognitive abilities, problem-solving skills, and executive functioning. These interventions also provide individuals with the tools and strategies they need to navigate the cognitive challenges associated with ASD and succeed in various areas of life.

Social Skills Interventions for Autism Spectrum Disorder

Social skills interventions are designed to help individuals with ASD develop the social skills they need to interact effectively with others. These interventions focus on teaching individuals how to understand social cues, initiate and maintain conversations, and develop meaningful relationships.

There are several examples of social skills interventions that can be effective for individuals with ASD. One example is social skills training, which involves teaching individuals specific social skills through modeling, role-playing, and practice. Another example is peer-mediated interventions, which involve pairing individuals with ASD with typically developing peers to facilitate social interactions.

Social skills interventions have been shown to have many benefits for individuals with ASD. They can improve social interactions, communication skills, and overall quality of life. These interventions also provide individuals with the tools and strategies they need to navigate social situations effectively and form meaningful relationships.

Communication Interventions for Autism Spectrum Disorder

Communication interventions are designed to help individuals with ASD improve their communication skills and abilities. These interventions focus on teaching individuals how to express themselves verbally or non-verbally, understand spoken language, and use alternative forms of communication.

There are several examples of communication interventions that can be effective for individuals with ASD. One example is speech therapy, which focuses on improving speech and language skills through various techniques and strategies. Another example is augmentative and alternative communication (AAC), which involves using tools and devices to support communication.

Communication interventions have been shown to have many benefits for individuals with ASD. They can improve communication skills, expressive and receptive language abilities, and overall quality of life. These interventions also provide individuals with the tools and strategies they need to effectively communicate their wants, needs, and thoughts.

Sensory Interventions for Autism Spectrum Disorder

Sensory interventions are designed to help individuals with ASD manage sensory sensitivities and challenges. Many individuals with ASD have heightened or diminished sensory responses, which can affect their ability to function in everyday environments. Sensory interventions aim to provide individuals with strategies to regulate their sensory experiences and navigate sensory-rich environments.

There are several examples of sensory interventions that can be effective for individuals with ASD. One example is sensory integration therapy, which involves engaging individuals in activities that stimulate their senses in a controlled and structured manner. Another example is the use of sensory tools such as weighted blankets or fidget toys to provide sensory input.

Sensory interventions have been shown to have many benefits for individuals with ASD. They can help individuals regulate their sensory experiences, reduce anxiety and stress, and improve overall functioning. These interventions also provide individuals with the tools and strategies they need to navigate sensory-rich environments more effectively.

Technology-Based Interventions for Autism Spectrum Disorder

Technology-based interventions are becoming increasingly popular in the treatment of Autism Spectrum Disorder. These interventions utilize technology such as computers, tablets, or smartphones to deliver therapeutic content and support individuals with ASD in various areas.

There are several examples of technology-based interventions that can be effective for individuals with ASD. One example is the use of social skills apps or programs that provide interactive and engaging activities to teach social skills. Another example is the use of virtual reality to create simulated environments for individuals to practice real-life situations.

Technology-based interventions have been shown to have many benefits for individuals with ASD. They can provide engaging and interactive learning experiences, increase motivation and participation, and improve overall outcomes. These interventions also provide individuals with the tools and strategies they need to navigate various areas of life using technology.

Medication-Based Interventions for Autism Spectrum Disorder

Medication-based interventions are sometimes used in the treatment of Autism Spectrum Disorder to manage specific symptoms or co-occurring conditions. These interventions aim to alleviate symptoms such as anxiety, hyperactivity, or aggression that may be interfering with an individual's functioning and well-being.

There are several examples of medication-based interventions that can be used for individuals with ASD. One example is the use of selective serotonin reuptake inhibitors (SSRIs) to manage anxiety or depression. Another example is the use of stimulant medications to manage hyperactivity or impulsivity.

Medication-based interventions can have benefits for individuals with ASD by reducing specific symptoms that may be interfering with their daily functioning. However, it is important to note that medication should always be used in conjunction with other interventions and under the guidance of a healthcare professional. There are potential risks and side effects associated with medication use, so it is important to carefully weigh the benefits and risks before making a decision.

The Future of Advanced Interventions for Autism Spectrum Disorder

The field of advanced interventions for Autism Spectrum Disorder is constantly evolving, and there is ongoing research and development in this area. Researchers are exploring new approaches and technologies to improve outcomes for individuals with ASD and address their unique challenges.

One area of current research is the use of virtual reality (VR) as a therapeutic tool for individuals with ASD. VR can provide immersive and realistic experiences that allow individuals to practice real-life situations in a controlled and safe environment. This can be particularly beneficial for individuals with ASD who struggle with social interactions or sensory sensitivities.

Another area of research is the use of genetic testing to identify specific genetic markers associated with ASD. This can help healthcare professionals develop personalized interventions based on an individual's genetic profile, leading to more targeted and effective treatments.

Continued research and development of interventions for ASD is crucial to improve outcomes and quality of life for individuals with this disorder. By staying up-to-date with the latest advancements in the field, individuals with ASD and their families can make informed decisions about the interventions that may be most beneficial for them.

Seeking advanced interventions for individuals with Autism Spectrum Disorder is crucial because it can greatly improve their overall well-being and development. These interventions are designed to address the specific challenges faced by individuals with ASD and provide them with the support and tools they need to thrive.

Early intervention and diagnosis are particularly important because they can lead to better outcomes for individuals with ASD. By addressing the challenges associated with ASD early on, individuals can have a better chance of reaching their full potential and leading fulfilling lives.

There are various types of advanced interventions available for individuals with ASD, including behavioral, cognitive, social skills, communication, sensory, technology-based, and medication-based interventions. Each type of intervention targets specific areas of challenge and provides individuals with the tools and strategies they need to navigate those challenges effectively.

The future of advanced interventions for Autism Spectrum Disorder looks promising, with ongoing research and development in the field. Researchers are exploring new approaches and technologies to improve outcomes for individuals with ASD and address their unique challenges.

In conclusion, seeking advanced interventions for individuals with Autism Spectrum Disorder is crucial because it can make a significant difference in their overall well-being and development. By addressing the specific challenges associated with ASD and providing targeted support, individuals can have a better chance of reaching their full potential and leading fulfilling lives. It is important for individuals with ASD and their families to seek professional help for diagnosis and intervention to ensure they receive the support and resources they need.

Chapter 5: Autism Beyond Childhood: Challenges and Triumphs for Adults

Autism Spectrum Disorder (ASD) is a neurodevelopmental disorder that affects individuals in various ways. It is characterized by difficulties in social communication and interaction, as well as restricted and repetitive patterns of behavior, interests, or activities. While much attention has been given to children with ASD, it is equally important to understand and support adults with ASD.

Statistics on the prevalence of ASD in adults vary, but it is estimated that around 1% of the global population has ASD. However, the number of adults diagnosed with ASD may be underreported due to late or missed diagnoses. Many individuals may not receive a diagnosis until adulthood, which can make it challenging for them to access appropriate support and services.

Understanding and supporting adults with ASD is crucial for their overall well-being and quality of life. By recognizing their unique strengths and challenges, we can create a more inclusive society that values and supports individuals with ASD.

Understanding the Unique Challenges of Autism in Adulthood

Adults with ASD face a range of challenges that can impact their daily lives. These challenges include differences in social communication and interaction, sensory processing difficulties, executive functioning challenges, and co-occurring mental health conditions.

Social communication and interaction can be particularly challenging for adults with ASD. They may struggle with understanding social cues, maintaining eye contact, or engaging in reciprocal conversations. This can lead to difficulties in forming and maintaining relationships, both personal and professional.

Sensory processing difficulties are also common among adults with ASD. They may be hypersensitive or hyposensitive to certain sensory stimuli, such as noise, touch, or light. This can result in sensory overload or sensory seeking behaviors, which can be overwhelming and distressing.

Executive functioning refers to a set of cognitive processes that help individuals plan, organize, and complete tasks. Adults with ASD often struggle with executive functioning challenges, such as time management, organization, and problem-solving. These difficulties can impact their ability to navigate daily tasks and responsibilities.

Additionally, many adults with ASD also experience co-occurring mental health conditions, such as anxiety and depression. These conditions can further complicate their daily lives and require additional support and intervention.

Navigating Relationships and Social Interactions

Building and maintaining relationships can be challenging for adults with ASD, but there are strategies that can help. It is important to provide individuals with opportunities for social interaction and practice social skills. This can be done through structured social skills training programs or by participating in group activities or clubs that align with their interests.

Coping with social anxiety and sensory overload in social situations is another important aspect of navigating relationships. Adults with ASD may benefit from developing coping strategies, such as deep breathing exercises or taking breaks when feeling overwhelmed. It is also important for individuals to communicate their needs and boundaries to others, so they can feel more comfortable in social settings.

There are resources available for social skills training and support. Many organizations offer social skills groups or workshops specifically designed for individuals with ASD. These programs provide a safe and supportive environment for individuals to practice social skills and build relationships.

Finding Employment and Career Success

Finding employment and achieving career success can be challenging for adults with ASD due to the unique difficulties they face. Many individuals with ASD have strengths in areas such as attention to detail, problem-solving, and pattern recognition, which can be valuable in certain careers.

However, there are also challenges that adults with ASD may encounter in the workplace. These challenges include difficulties with social communication, sensory sensitivities, and executive functioning. It is important for employers to provide accommodations and supports to help individuals with ASD succeed on the job.

Accommodations can include providing a quiet workspace, allowing flexible work hours, or providing clear instructions and expectations. Employers can also offer training programs or mentorship opportunities to help individuals with ASD develop their skills and advance in their careers.

There are resources available for job training and employment assistance for individuals with ASD. Vocational rehabilitation programs, job coaches, and disability employment services can provide support and guidance in finding and maintaining employment.

Managing Sensory Overload in the Workplace

Sensory overload can be a significant challenge for adults with ASD in the workplace. Common triggers for sensory overload include loud noises, bright lights, strong smells, or crowded spaces. Sensory overload can lead to anxiety, stress, and difficulty concentrating.

There are strategies that individuals with ASD can use to manage sensory overload in the workplace. This may include using noise-canceling headphones, taking regular breaks in a quiet space, or using fidget toys to help regulate sensory input. It is important for individuals to communicate their needs to their employers and advocate for accommodations that can help them manage sensory overload.

Advocating for accommodations and modifications in the workplace is crucial for individuals with ASD. This may involve having open and honest conversations with employers or human resources departments about specific needs and challenges. By advocating for their needs, individuals with ASD can create a more supportive and inclusive work environment.

Coping with Anxiety and Depression

Anxiety and depression are common co-occurring mental health conditions among adults with ASD. The prevalence of anxiety and depression in this population is higher than in the general population. These conditions can significantly impact an individual's daily life and overall well-being.

There are strategies that individuals with ASD can use to manage anxiety and depression. These strategies may include practicing relaxation techniques, engaging in regular exercise, seeking therapy or counseling, or participating in support groups. It is important for individuals to reach out for professional help if needed and to develop a support network of friends, family, or peers who can provide emotional support.

There are resources available for mental health support for adults with ASD. Many organizations offer therapy services specifically tailored to individuals with ASD. These services can provide individuals with the tools and strategies they need to manage their anxiety and depression effectively.

Accessing Healthcare and Support Services

Accessing healthcare and support services can be challenging for adults with ASD. Many individuals face barriers such as lack of understanding from healthcare providers, limited access to specialized services, or difficulties navigating the healthcare system.

It is important for individuals with ASD to advocate for their healthcare and support needs. This may involve educating healthcare providers about their specific needs and challenges, seeking out specialized services or providers who have experience working with individuals with ASD, or reaching out to advocacy organizations for guidance and support.

There are resources available for finding and accessing appropriate healthcare and support services. Autism advocacy organizations can provide information and resources on healthcare providers, support groups, or other services that may be beneficial for adults with ASD.

Building Independent Living Skills

Developing independent living skills is crucial for adults with ASD to live fulfilling and independent lives. These skills include tasks such as managing finances, cooking, cleaning, personal hygiene, and transportation.

Strategies for building independent living skills may include breaking tasks down into smaller steps, using visual supports or schedules, practicing skills in a structured environment, or seeking out training programs or classes that focus on independent living skills.

There are resources available for independent living support. Many organizations offer programs or services specifically designed to help individuals with ASD develop independent living skills. These programs can provide guidance, support, and practical tools to help individuals become more self-sufficient.

Advocating for Autism Acceptance and Inclusion

Advocating for autism acceptance and inclusion is crucial for creating a more inclusive society that values and supports individuals with ASD. It is important to challenge stereotypes and misconceptions about autism and promote understanding and acceptance.

There are many ways to get involved in advocacy efforts. This may include participating in awareness campaigns, supporting autism organizations through donations or volunteering, or sharing personal stories and experiences to promote positive representation of individuals with ASD.

There are resources available for advocacy and activism. Autism advocacy organizations can provide information, resources, and guidance on how to get involved in advocacy efforts. By working together, we can create a more inclusive and accepting society for individuals with ASD.

Celebrating the Triumphs and Achievements of Adults with Autism

It is important to celebrate the triumphs and achievements of adults with ASD. By highlighting their successes, we can challenge stereotypes and promote a more positive and inclusive narrative about autism.

There are many examples of successful adults with ASD who have made significant contributions in various fields. These individuals serve as role models and inspiration for others with ASD. By sharing their stories, we can promote positive representation and encourage others to pursue their goals and dreams.

There are resources available for sharing success stories and promoting positive representation. Many organizations and websites feature stories of individuals with ASD who have achieved success in various areas. These resources can provide inspiration and encouragement for individuals with ASD and their families.

The Importance of Supporting Adults with Autism

Understanding and supporting adults with ASD is crucial for their overall well-being and quality of life. By recognizing their unique strengths and challenges, we can create a more inclusive society that values and supports individuals with ASD.

Adults with ASD face a range of challenges, including differences in social communication and interaction, sensory processing difficulties, executive functioning challenges, and co-occurring mental health conditions. However, there are strategies, resources, and supports available to help them navigate these challenges and live fulfilling lives.

It is important for individuals with ASD to advocate for their needs, access appropriate support services, and develop independent living skills. By celebrating the triumphs and achievements of adults with ASD, we can challenge stereotypes and promote a more positive narrative about autism.

In conclusion, supporting adults with ASD is not only beneficial for individuals with ASD themselves but also for society as a whole. By creating a more inclusive and accepting society, we can ensure that individuals with ASD have the opportunities and support they need to thrive. It is our collective responsibility to understand, support, and advocate for adults with ASD.

Chapter 6: The Power of Play: Using Play Therapy to Support Children with Autism

Autism is a neurodevelopmental disorder that affects a child's social interaction, communication skills, and behavior. It is estimated that 1 in 54 children in the United States is diagnosed with autism spectrum disorder (ASD). Children with autism often face challenges in their development, including difficulties in socializing, communicating, and regulating their emotions. Play therapy has emerged as an effective intervention for children with autism, as it promotes social, emotional, and cognitive development.

Play is a fundamental aspect of childhood and is essential for the overall development of children. It provides opportunities for children to explore, learn, and develop important skills. For children with autism, play therapy offers a structured and supportive environment where they can engage in play activities that are specifically designed to address their unique needs and challenges.

Defining Play Therapy and its Benefits for Children with Autism

Play therapy is a therapeutic approach that uses play as a means of communication and expression. It is based on the understanding that play is a natural and instinctive way for children to make sense of their world and express their thoughts and feelings. The goals of play therapy for children with autism include improving communication skills, enhancing social interaction, promoting emotional regulation, and developing cognitive abilities.

One of the key benefits of play therapy for children with autism is improved communication. Many children with autism struggle with verbal communication and may have difficulty expressing themselves or understanding others. Through play therapy, children are encouraged to use various forms of communication, such as gestures, facial expressions, and body language. This helps them develop alternative means of communication and enhances their ability to understand and respond to others.

Another benefit of play therapy for children with autism is the improvement in social skills. Children with autism often struggle with social interaction and may find it challenging to initiate or maintain conversations, make eye contact, or understand social cues. Play therapy provides a safe and structured environment where children can practice social skills, such as turn-taking, sharing, and cooperation. It also helps them learn how to read social cues and understand the perspectives of others.

Emotional regulation is another area where play therapy can be beneficial for children with autism. Many children with autism have difficulty managing their emotions and may experience meltdowns or become overwhelmed in certain situations. Play therapy allows children to explore and express their emotions in a safe and supportive environment. Through play, they can learn strategies for self-regulation, such as deep breathing or using calming techniques.

The Role of Play in Developing Social and Communication Skills in Children with Autism

Play plays a crucial role in the development of social and communication skills in children with autism. It provides opportunities for children to practice and learn important social cues, such as eye contact, body language, and facial expressions. Through play, children can also develop their communication skills by using gestures, sounds, or words to express their thoughts and feelings.

One example of a play activity that promotes social and communication development is pretend play. Pretend play involves children taking on different roles and engaging in imaginary scenarios. This type of play allows children to practice social skills, such as turn-taking, sharing, and cooperation. It also encourages them to use their imagination and creativity to communicate and problem-solve.

Another example of a play activity that promotes social and communication development is board games or card games. These games require children to take turns, follow rules, and communicate with others. They provide opportunities for children to practice important social skills, such as waiting for their turn, listening to others, and expressing their thoughts or opinions.

How Play Therapy Helps Children with Autism Build Self-Esteem and Confidence

Play therapy can play a significant role in promoting self-esteem and confidence in children with autism. Many children with autism struggle with low self-esteem due to difficulties in socializing, communicating, or understanding social cues. Play therapy provides a safe and supportive environment where children can engage in activities that build their self-esteem and confidence.

One way play therapy promotes self-esteem and confidence is by allowing children to experience success and mastery. In play therapy, activities are carefully designed to match the child's abilities and interests, ensuring that they can succeed and feel a sense of accomplishment. This helps boost their self-esteem and confidence in their abilities.

Another way play therapy promotes self-esteem and confidence is by providing opportunities for children to make choices and have control over their play experiences. In play therapy, children are encouraged to make decisions, express their preferences, and take the lead in their play activities. This helps them develop a sense of autonomy and empowerment, which can positively impact their self-esteem and confidence.

The Different Types of Play Therapy Approaches for Children with Autism

There are different approaches to play therapy that can be used with children with autism. These approaches can be categorized into structured and unstructured play therapy.

Structured play therapy involves the use of specific play activities or interventions that are designed to target specific goals or skills. These activities are often guided by a therapist or caregiver who provides support, guidance, and feedback. Structured play therapy can include activities such as sensory play, art therapy, music therapy, or social skills groups.

Unstructured play therapy, on the other hand, allows children to engage in free play without specific goals or interventions. It provides a more open-ended and child-led approach to play therapy. Unstructured play therapy can include activities such as playing with toys, building blocks, engaging in imaginative play, or exploring nature.

Both structured and unstructured play therapy approaches have their benefits for children with autism. Structured play therapy provides a more focused and targeted approach to addressing specific goals or challenges. It allows therapists or caregivers to provide support and guidance in a structured environment. On the other hand, unstructured play therapy allows children to explore and express themselves freely. It encourages creativity, imagination, and self-expression.

The Importance of Tailoring Play Therapy to Meet the Unique Needs of Each Child with Autism

It is essential to tailor play therapy to meet the unique needs and interests of each child with autism. Every child with autism is different and has their own strengths, challenges, and preferences. By tailoring play therapy to meet each child's individual needs, therapists and caregivers can create a more effective and engaging therapeutic experience.

One strategy for tailoring play therapy is to incorporate the child's interests into the play activities. For example, if a child is interested in dinosaurs, the therapist or caregiver can use dinosaur toys or books during play therapy sessions. This not only captures the child's attention but also provides opportunities for learning and engagement.

Another strategy for tailoring play therapy is to consider the child's sensory preferences. Many children with autism have sensory sensitivities or preferences. Some may be sensitive to certain textures, sounds, or smells, while others may seek out sensory input. By understanding and accommodating these sensory preferences, therapists and caregivers can create a more comfortable and enjoyable play therapy experience for the child.

Strategies for Encouraging Play and Engagement in Children with Autism

Encouraging play and engagement in children with autism can sometimes be challenging. However, there are strategies that parents and caregivers can use to promote play and engagement in children with autism.

One strategy is to create a structured and predictable environment for play. Children with autism often thrive in environments that are organized, consistent, and predictable. By creating a designated play area with clear boundaries and rules, parents and caregivers can help children feel more comfortable and engaged in play.

Another strategy is to provide visual supports during play. Many children with autism are visual learners and benefit from visual cues or supports. Parents and caregivers can use visual schedules, visual prompts, or visual timers to help children understand and follow the rules or expectations of play.

Adapting play activities to meet the child's needs and interests is another effective strategy. For example, if a child has difficulty with fine motor skills, parents and caregivers can provide adapted toys or tools that are easier to manipulate. If a child has a special interest in trains, parents and caregivers can incorporate train-themed activities into play.

The Role of Parents and Caregivers in Supporting Play Therapy for Children with Autism

Parents and caregivers play a crucial role in supporting play therapy for children with autism. They are the child's primary caregivers and have a unique understanding of their child's strengths, challenges, and preferences. By actively participating in play therapy and implementing strategies at home, parents and caregivers can enhance the effectiveness of play therapy.

One important role of parents and caregivers is to provide a supportive and nurturing environment for play therapy. This includes creating a safe and comfortable space for play, setting aside dedicated time for play therapy sessions, and being actively engaged in the child's play activities.

Another role of parents and caregivers is to reinforce the skills learned in play therapy at home. This can be done by incorporating the strategies or techniques used in play therapy into everyday routines or activities. For example, if the child learned a calming technique during play therapy, parents can encourage the child to use it when they are feeling overwhelmed or anxious.

Parents and caregivers can also collaborate with the play therapist to set goals and monitor progress. By maintaining open communication with the play therapist, parents can stay informed about their child's progress in play therapy and work together to address any challenges or concerns that may arise.

The Benefits of Play Therapy for the Entire Family of a Child with Autism

Play therapy not only benefits the child with autism but also has positive effects on the entire family. It can improve family relationships, communication, and overall well-being.

One benefit of play therapy for the family is improved communication. Play therapy provides a safe and supportive environment where family members can engage in play activities together. This can help improve communication and understanding between family members, as they learn to listen, respond, and interact with each other in a playful and non-threatening way.

Play therapy can also improve family relationships by promoting bonding and connection. Engaging in play activities together allows family members to spend quality time with each other, creating opportunities for shared experiences and positive interactions. This can strengthen the parent-child relationship, as well as sibling relationships.

Furthermore, play therapy can have a positive impact on the overall well-being of the family. It provides a space for families to relax, have fun, and reduce stress. Play therapy can also help parents and caregivers develop new strategies and techniques for supporting their child with autism, which can lead to increased confidence and reduced feelings of overwhelm.

Addressing Challenges and Limitations in Using Play Therapy for Children with Autism

While play therapy is a valuable intervention for children with autism, there are some challenges and limitations that need to be addressed.

One common challenge is the difficulty in engaging children with autism in play activities. Some children with autism may have limited interests or preferences, making it challenging to find activities that capture their attention. In such cases, therapists and caregivers may need to be creative and adapt play activities to match the child's interests or sensory preferences.

Another challenge is the need for ongoing support and consistency. Play therapy is most effective when it is provided consistently over time. However, it can be challenging for parents and caregivers to maintain regular play therapy sessions at home or find qualified therapists who specialize in working with children with autism. It is important for parents and caregivers to seek out resources and support networks that can provide guidance and assistance in implementing play therapy.

The Ongoing Importance of Play Therapy in Supporting Children with Autism

In conclusion, play therapy is a valuable intervention for children with autism. It promotes social, emotional, and cognitive development and helps children with autism improve their communication skills, social interaction, and emotional regulation. Play therapy can be tailored to meet the unique needs and interests of each child with autism, and it is important for parents, caregivers, and professionals to prioritize play therapy in supporting children with autism. By understanding the importance of play and implementing strategies to support play therapy, we can help children with autism thrive and reach their full potential.

Don't miss out!

Visit the website below and you can sign up to receive emails whenever Travis Breeding publishes a new book. There's no charge and no obligation.

https://books2read.com/r/B-A-CBXDB-DWDXC

BOOKS 2 READ

Connecting independent readers to independent writers.

Did you love *Breaking Barriers: Navigating Autism With Therapeutic Insight*? Then you should read *Celebrating Neurodiversity*[1] by Travis Breeding!

[2]

"Celebrating Neurodiversity" is not just a book; it's a manifesto for acceptance, understanding, and inclusivity. Breeding passionately advocates for the celebration of differences, urging readers to embrace the mosaic of neurodiversity that enriches our society. Through empowering stories of resilience, creativity, and innovation, Breeding showcases the immense potential that lies within the neurodivergent community.

From the unique ways in which neurodivergent individuals perceive the world to the invaluable insights they offer, "Celebrating Neurodiversity" is a thought-provoking exploration of what it truly

---

1. https://books2read.com/u/4DnjxP

2. https://books2read.com/u/4DnjxP

means to be neurodivergent. Breeding's empowering narrative inspires readers to challenge preconceived notions, foster empathy, and champion diversity in all its forms.

Whether you're a neurodivergent individual, a caregiver, or simply curious about the intricacies of the human mind, "Celebrating Neurodiversity" is a must-read that will leave a lasting impact. Join Travis Breeding on a journey of self-discovery, acceptance, and celebration as we embrace the kaleidoscope of neurodiversity and revel in the beauty of our differences.

Read more at breedingautismconsulting.com.

Also by Travis Breeding

Harmony in Flux: Navigating Bi-Polar Brilliance
The Friendship Rainbow
The Great Kindergarten Adventure: A Story about Going to School
with Autism
The Magic Forest Adventure
Unlocking Brilliance: Navigating Autism and Applied Behavior
Analysis Towards a Radiant Future
Decoding Love: Navigating Dating and Relationships on the Autism
Spectrum
Echoes of a Late Diagnosis: Unveiling the Spectrum Within
From Theory to Practice: Implementing Effective Autism Interventions
St
The Amazing Adventures of Aiden and His Asperger's Superpowers
The Magical Adventures of Lily and the Enchanted Forest
Unlocking Potential: A Journey Of Discovery Through ABA Therapy
Unlocking Potential: Navigating Employment for Neurodiverse Talent
Unlocking the Spectrum: A Journey through Applied Behavior Analysis
from an Autistic Perspective
Unlocking The Spectrum: Navigating The Complexity Of Autism With
Advanced Strategies And Insights
Beyond The Spectrum: Insights From Autistic Adults
Beyond The Stereotypes
Breaking Barriers: Navigating Autism With Therapeutic Insight
Celebrating Neurodiversity
Embracing Differences

From Diagnosis To Treatment
From Dreams To Reality: The Young President
Living With Autism: A Journey Of Triumph And Challenges
Neurodiversity Unveiled: Navigating The Spectrum Of Inclusion
The Art Of Reinforcement
ThroughThe Spectrum Of Love

Watch for more at breedingautismconsulting.com.

About the Author

Travis is the author of over 50 books about autism spectrum disorder. He travelst he country sharing the mission of making the world a better place for autistic individuals. In his spare time Travis enjoys writing, walking, and watching sports.

Read more at breedingautismconsulting.com.